T0037039

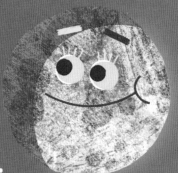

WHEN
MOON
BECAME THE
MOON

ROB HODGSON

RISE
NEW YORK

For Sue & Lou

—RH

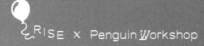

RISE × Penguin Workshop

An imprint of Penguin Random House LLC, New York

First published in the United States of America by Rise × Penguin Workshop,
an imprint of Penguin Random House LLC, New York, 2023

Visit us online at penguinrandomhouse.com.

Library of Congress Cataloging-in-Publication Data is available.

Manufactured in China

ISBN 9780593523629   10 9 8 7 6 5 4 3 2 1 HH

The text is set in AauxPro OT.
This art was created with traditional media and an iPad, and assembled in Photoshop.

Edited by Nicole Fox
Designed by Maria Elias

CONTENTS

CHAPTER 1

SUN

Space is a very, very big place.

It is home to billions of stars.

One of those stars is our Sun.

I'm a super star!

Long ago, eight planets formed
around Sun. He loved to share
his light and warmth with them.

Hey, neighbors!

CHAPTER 2

EARTH

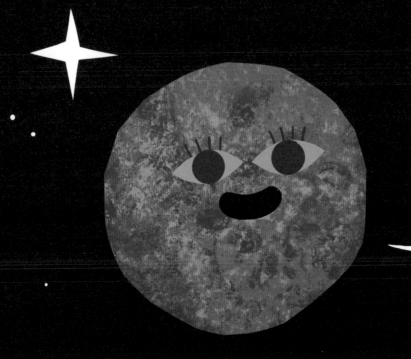

This is Earth, the third
closest planet to Sun.
She was still hot from forming,
but she already loved her place
in the neighborhood.

As the planets grew up, some moon friends began forming around them.

Earth wanted a moon friend, too.

Just one would be enough!

CHAPTER 3

BABY
MOON

Earth got to work: She and another
early planet crashed together.

Melting rocks went flying everywhere!

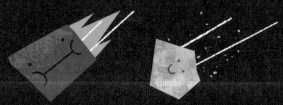

Then, Earth used a special force,
called gravity, to keep the rocks close by.

Some of the rocks were so excited to be
together that they got closer and closer,
and hotter and hotter, until . . .

They came together to form a moon!

CHAPTER 4

ORBIT

Earth and Moon were so
happy to be new friends.

They wanted to stay in space
together forever!

I'll never leave
your side!

Earth and Moon loved
to spin as they circled,
or orbited, around Sun
together.

Earth circled around Sun every year, and Moon circled around Earth every month. They loved their orbital journeys!

Day after day, and year after year,
Moon journeyed around Earth.

That was cool!

After billions of years, Moon and Earth
cooled down and changed colors!

CHAPTER 5

CRATERS

Moon changed in other ways, too.
Along her journey, she welcomed lots
of flying rocks from space.

When they landed on Moon,
they made different sized holes,
or craters, on her surface.

Moon loved all her craters.

MOON TODAY

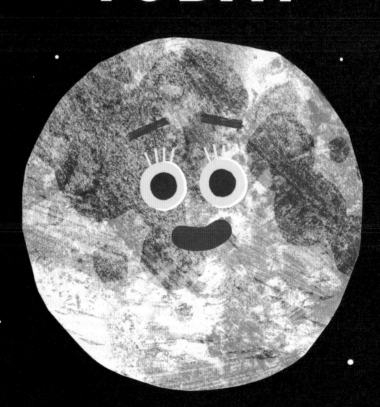

Moon looks a little different now
from when she first formed,
but she's still the same moon.

CHAPTER 6

LIGHT

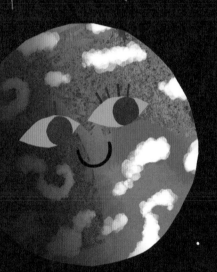

Look! It's our friend Sun.

Sun and Moon work together to light up
Earth's skies. Sun shines his light toward
Earth, and Moon reflects it.

They make a great team!

Thanks to Sun and Moon,
Earth gets lit with sunlight
during the day and moonlight
during the night!

You two light up my life!

CHAPTER 7

MOON PHASES

The moonlight Earth gets at night
isn't always the same, though.

It changes depending on where Moon is on her journey around Earth, and how much light her face is reflecting from Sun.

When my whole face is lit, I'm called a Full Moon!

A few days after being full, Moon's face—
that's the side of her we always see—gets less
light from Sun. Moon's face looks darker . . .

. . . and darker . . .

. . . and darker still.

At Moon's halfway point around Earth,
she only gets lit up from behind, making
Moon's face look invisible from Earth!

Psst . . . I'm still here, but now I'm called a New Moon!

As Moon continues circling around Earth,
her face starts to get more of Sun's light again.

She gets brighter . . .

. . . and brighter . . .

. . . and brighter still.

**Now I'm called
a Waxing Moon!**

Moon has gone full circle around Earth!

That was out of this world!

It was a long journey, and Moon's
excited to start it all over again!

CHAPTER 8

MOON HELPS EARTH

During each journey around Earth, Moon does some important things. One of them is to help make Earth's ocean tides.

Moon makes tides by using her gravity to pull some of Earth's water toward her, making high tides, and push some of Earth's water inward, making low tides.

On Earth, high tides make the ocean water
rise higher . . .

And low tides make the ocean water
sink lower.

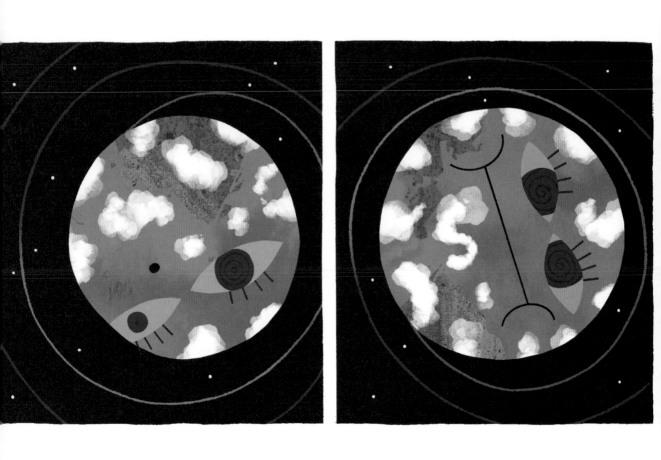

Moon also uses her gravity to keep Earth steady
when she wobbles.

After all, Moon and Earth
want to spin in orbit
together forever.

CHAPTER 9
SOLAR ECLIPSE

Once in a while, Moon likes to do a special "magic" trick during Earth's daytime.

Moon moves in front of Sun,
blocking out his light.

For a few minutes, Earth's sky gets . . .

DARK!

Whoa!

Then Moon moves back over
and it's daytime again!

CHAPTER 10

VISITORS

Moon continues her journey,
reflecting Sun's light
onto Earth.

All the while, the people of Earth
look up to see and admire her.

People love Moon so much,
that some have worked very hard
to learn more about her!

People have walked on Moon,
sent rovers to study her . . .

and some have plans
to visit her again soon.

Hello over there!

CHAPTER 11

THE
FUTURE

Moon sure does love being a moon.

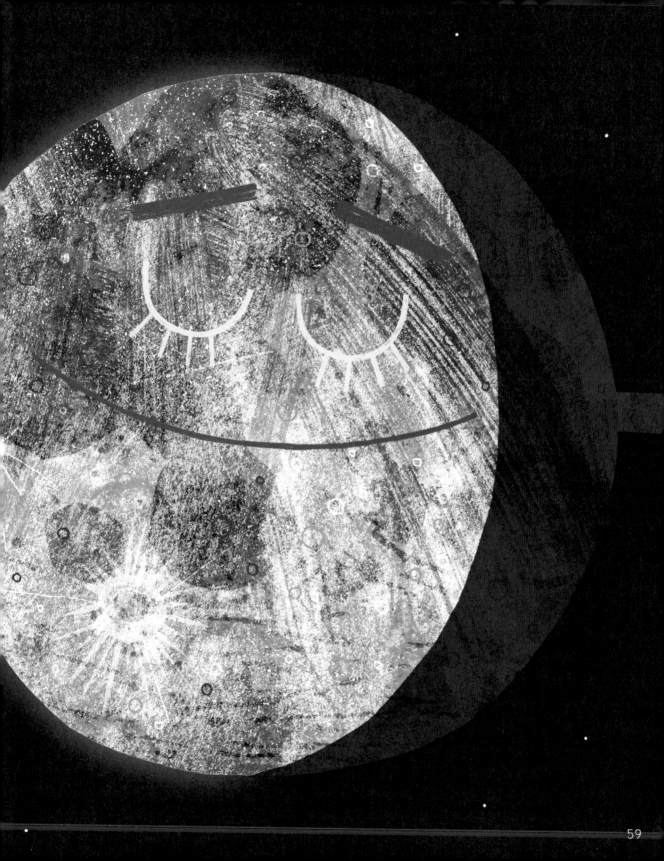

She looks forward to continuing
her journey over billions of years,

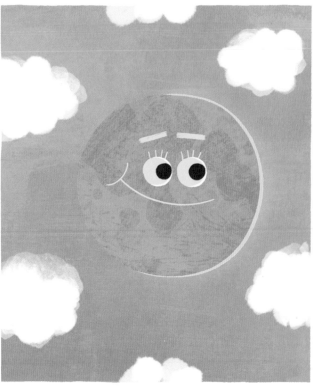

lighting Earth's night sky along the way,

I'll always be your night-light!

making the ocean tides,

keeping Earth steady,
and someday meeting more
visitors.

But most of all, Moon can't wait to look down from her spot in the night sky and see you, her new friend!

Come visit me someday!